Homage to Mistress Bradstreet

AND OTHER POEMS

JOHN BERRYMAN

Homage to Mistress Bradstreet

AND

Other Poems

Farrar, Straus & Giroux

NEW YORK

Note

The present volume is being issued at the request of my publisher in order to make available in an inexpensive edition the text of *Homage to Mistress Bradstreet* and some of my short poems. This volume contains, besides the title poem (1953 in *Partisan Review*; 1956 in book form), a selection from *The Dispossessed* (1948), which drew on two earlier collections, some poems from *His Thought Made Pockets & The Plane Buckt* (1958) and one poem from *Sonnets* (1967). None of the *Dream Songs* is included.

J. B.

Contents

Homage to Mistress Bradstreet
AND OTHER POEMS

[Born 1612 Anne Dudley, married at 16 Simon Bradstreet, a Cambridge man, steward to the Countess of Warwick and protégé of her father Thomas Dudley secretary to the Earl of Lincoln. Crossed in the *Arbella*, 1630, under Governor Winthrop.]

Homage to Mistress Bradstreet

1

The Governor your husband lived so long
moved you not, restless, waiting for him? Still,
you were a patient woman—
I seem to see you pause here still:
Sylvester, Quarles, in moments odd you pored
before a fire at, bright eyes on the Lord,
all the children still.
'Simon . .' Simon will listen while you read a Song.

2

Outside the New World winters in grand dark
white air lashing high thro' the virgin stands
foxes down foxholes sigh,
surely the English heart quails, stunned.
I doubt if Simon than this blast, that sea,
spares from his rigour for your poetry
more. We are on each other's hands
who care. Both of our worlds unhanded us. Lie stark,

3

thy eyes look to me mild. Out of maize & air
your body's made, and moves. I summon, see,
from the centuries it.
I think you won't stay. How do we
linger, diminished, in our lovers' air,
implausibly visible, to whom, a year,
years, over interims; or not;
to a long stranger; or not; shimmer and disappear.

4

Jaw-ript, rot with its wisdom, rending then;
then not. When the mouth dies, who misses you?
Your master never died,
Simon ah thirty years past you —
Pockmarkt & westward staring on a haggard deck
it seems I find you, young. I come to check,
I come to stay with you,
and the Governor, & Father, & Simon, & the huddled men.

5

By the week we landed we were, most, used up.
Strange ships across us, after a fortnight's winds
unfavouring, frightened us;
bone-sad cold, sleet, scurvy; so were ill
many as one day we could have no sermons;
broils, quelled; a fatherless child unkennelled; vermin
crowding & waiting: waiting.
And the day itself he leapt ashore young Henry Winthrop

6

(delivered from the waves; because he found
off their wigwams, sharp-eyed, a lone canoe
across a tidal river,
that water glittered fair & blue
& narrow, none of the other men could swim
and the plantation's prime theft up to him,
shouldered on a glad day
hard on the glorious feasting of thanksgiving) drowned.

7

How long with nothing in the ruinous heat,
clams & acorns stomaching, distinction perishing,
at which my heart rose,
with brackish water, we would sing.
When whispers knew the Governor's last bread
was browning in his oven, we were discourag'd.
The Lady Arbella dying —
dyings — at which my heart   rose, but I did submit.

8

That beyond the Atlantic wound our woes enlarge
is hard, hard that starvation burnishes our fear,
but I do gloss for You.
Strangers & pilgrims fare we here,
declaring we seek a City. Shall we be deceived?
I know whom I have trusted, & whom I have believed,
and that he is able to
keep   that I have committed to his charge.

9

Winter than summer worse, that first, like a file
on a quick, or the poison suck of a thrilled tooth;
and still we may unpack.
Wolves & storms among, uncouth
board-pieces, boxes, barrels vanish, grow
houses, rise. Motes that hop in sunlight slow
indoors, and I am Ruth
away: open my mouth, my eyes wet: I would smile:

vellum I palm, and dream. Their forest dies
to greensward, privets, elms & towers, whence
a nightingale is throbbing.
Women sleep sound. I was happy once . .
(Something keeps on not happening; I shrink?)
These minutes all their passions & powers sink
and I am not one chance
for an unknown cry or a flicker of unknown eyes.

Chapped souls ours, by the day Spring's strong winds swelled,
Jack's pulpits arched, more glad. The shawl I pinned
flaps like a shooting soul
might in such weather Heaven send.
Succumbing half, in spirit, to a salmon sash
I prod the nerveless novel succotash —
I must be disciplined,
in arms, against that one, and our dissidents, and myself.

Versing, I shroud among the dynasties;
quaternion on quaternion, tireless I phrase
anything past, dead, far,
sacred, for a barbarous place.
—To please your wintry father? all this bald
abstract didactic rime I read appalled
harassed for your fame
mistress neither of fiery nor velvet verse, on your knees

hopeful & shamefast, chaste, laborious, odd,
whom the sea tore.—The damned roar with loss,
so they hug & are mean
with themselves, and I cannot be thus.
Why then do I repine, sick, bad, to long
after what must not be? I lie wrong
once more. For at fourteen
I found my heart more carnal and sitting loose from God,

vanity & the follies of youth took hold of me;
then the pox blasted, when the Lord returned.
That year for my sorry face
so-much-older Simon burned,
so Father smiled, with love. Their will be done.
He to me ill lingeringly, learning to shun
a bliss, a lightning blood
vouchsafed, what did seem life. I kissed his Mystery.

Drydust in God's eye the aquavivid skin
of Simon snoring lit with fountaining dawn
when my eyes unlid, sad.
John Cotton shines on Boston's sin —
I ám drawn, in pieties that seem
the weary drizzle of an unremembered dream.
Women have gone mad
at twenty-one. Ambition mines, atrocious, in.

16

Food endless, people few, all to be done.
As pippins roast, the question of the wolves
turns & turns.
Fangs of a wolf will keep, the neck
round of a child, that child brave. I remember who
in meeting smiled & was punisht, and I know who
whispered & was stockt.
We lead a thoughtful life. But Boston's cage we shun.

17

The winters close, Springs open, no child stirs
under my withering heart, O seasoned heart
God grudged his aid.
All things else soil like a shirt.
Simon is much away. My executive stales.
The town came through for the cartway by the pales,
but my patience is short,
I revolt from, I am like, these savage foresters

18

whose passionless dicker in the shade, whose glance
impassive & scant, belie their murderous cries
when quarry seems to show.
Again I must have been wrong, twice.
Unwell in a new way. Can that begin?
God brandishes. O love, O I love. Kin,
gather. My world is strange
and merciful, ingrown months, blessing a swelling trance.

19

So squeezed, wince you I scream? I love you & hate
off with you. Ages! *Useless.* Below my waist
he has me in Hell's vise.
Stalling. He let go. Come back: brace
me somewhere. No. No. Yes! everything down
hardens I press with horrible joy down
my back cracks like a wrist
shame I am voiding oh behind it is too late

20

hide me forever I work thrust I must free
now I all muscles & bones concentrate
what is living from dying?
Simon I must leave you so untidy
Monster you are killing me Be sure
I'll have you later Women do endure
I can *can* no longer
and it passes the wretched trap whelming and I am me

21

drencht & powerful, I did it with my body!
One proud tug greens Heaven. Marvellous,
unforbidding Majesty.
Swell, imperious bells. I fly.
Mountainous, woman not breaks and will bend:
sways God nearby: anguish comes to an end.
Blossomed Sarah, and I
blossom. Is that thing alive? I hear a famisht howl.

Beloved household, I am Simon's wife,
and the mother of Samuel — whom greedy yet I miss
out of his kicking place.
More in some ways I feel at a loss,
freer. Cantabanks & mummers, nears
longing for you. Our chopping scores my ears,
our costume bores my eyes.
St. George to the good sword, rise! chop-logic's rife

& fever & Satan & Satan's ancient fere.
Pioneering is not feeling well,
not Indians, beasts.
Not all their riddling can forestall
one leaving. Sam, your uncle has had to
go frŏm us to live with God. 'Then Aunt went too?'
Dear, she does wait still.
Stricken: 'Oh. Then he takes   us one by one.' My dear.

Forswearing it otherwise, they starch their minds.
Folkmoots, & blether, blether. John Cotton rakes
to the synod of Cambridge.
Down from my body my legs flow,
out from it arms wave, on it my head shakes.
Now Mistress Hutchinson rings forth a call —
should she? many creep out at a broken wall —
affirming the Holy Ghost
dwells in one justified. Factioning passion blinds

all to all her good, all — can she be exiled?
Bitter sister, victim! I miss you.
— I miss you, Anne,
day or night weak as a child,
tender & empty, doomed, quick to no tryst.
— I hear you. Be kind, you who leaguer
my image in the mist.
— Be kind you, to one unchained eager far & wild

and if, O my love, my heart is breaking, please
neglect my cries and I will spare you. Deep
in Time's grave, Love's, you lie still.
Lie still. — Now? That happy shape
my forehead had under my most long, rare,
ravendark, hidden, soft bodiless hair
you award me still.
You must not love me, but   I do not bid you cease.

Veiled my eyes, attending. How can it be I?
Moist, with parted lips, I listen, wicked.
I shake in the morning & retch.
Brood I do on myself naked.
A fading world I dust, with fingers new.
— I have earned the right to be alone with you.
— What right can that be?
Convulsing, if you love, enough, like a sweet lie.

28

Not that, I know, you can. This cratered skin,
like the crabs & shells of my Palissy ewer, touch!
Oh, you do, you do?
Falls on me what I like a witch,
for lawless holds, annihilations of law
which Time and he and man abhor, foresaw:
sharper than what my Friend
brought me for my revolt when I moved smooth & thin,

29

faintings black, rigour, chilling, brown
parching, back, brain burning, the grey pocks
itch, a manic stench
of pustules snapping, pain floods the palm,
sleepless, or a red shaft with a dreadful start
rides at the chapel, like a slipping heart.
My soul strains in one qualm
ah but *this* is not to save me but to throw me down.

30

And out of this I lull. It lessens. Kiss me.
That once. As sings out up in sparkling dark
a trail of a star & dies,
while the breath flutters, sounding, mark,
so shorn ought such caresses to us be
who, deserving nothing, flush and flee
the darkness of that light,
a lurching frozen from a warm dream. Talk to me.

—It is Spring's New England. Pussy willows wedge
up in the wet. Milky crestings, fringed
yellow, in heaven, eyed
by the melting hand-in-hand or mere
desirers single, heavy-footed, rapt,
make surge poor human hearts. Venus is trapt —
the hefty pike shifts, sheer —
in Orion blazing. Warblings, odours, nudge to an edge —

— Ravishing, ha, what crouches outside ought,
flamboyant, ill, angelic. Often, now,
I am afraid of you.
I am a sobersides; I know.
I *want* to take you for my lover. — Do.
— I hear a madness. Harmless I to you
am not, not I? — No.
— I cannot but be. Sing a concord of our thought.

—Wan dolls in indigo on gold: refrain
my western lust. I am drowning in this past.
I lose sight of you
who mistress me from air. Unbraced
in delirium of the grand depths, giving away
haunters what kept me, I breathe solid spray.
— I am losing you!
Straiten me on. — I suffered living like a stain:

34

I trundle the bodies, on the iron bars,
over that fire backward & forth; they burn;
bits fall. I wonder if
I killed them. Women serve my turn.
— Dreams! You are good. — No. — Dense with hardihood
the wicked are dislodged, and lodged the good.
In green space we are safe.
God awaits us (but I am yielding) who Hell wars.

35

— I cannot feel myself God waits. He flies
nearer a kindly world; or he is flown.
One Saturday's rescue
won't show. Man is entirely alone
may be. I am a man of griefs & fits
trying to be my friend. And the brown smock splits,
down the pale flesh a gash
broadens and Time holds up your heart against my eyes.

36

— Hard and divided heaven! creases me. Shame
is failing. My breath is scented, and I throw
hostile glances towards God.
Crumpling plunge of a pestle, bray:
sin cross & opposite, wherein I survive
nightmares of Eden. Reaches foul & live
he for me, this soul
to crunch, a minute tangle of eternal flame.

37

I fear Hell's hammer-wind. But fear does wane.
Death's blossoms grain my hair; I cannot live.
A black joy clashes
joy, in twilight. The Devil said
'I will deal toward her softly, and her enchanting cries
will fool the horns of Adam.' Father of lies,
a male great pestle smashes
small women swarming towards the mortar's rim in vain.

38

I see the cruel spread Wings black with saints!
Silky my breasts not his, mine, mine to withhold
or tender, tender.
I am sifting, nervous, and bold.
The light is changing. Surrender this loveliness
you cannot make me do. *But* I will. Yes.
What horror, down stormy air,
warps towards me? My threatening promise faints

39

torture me, Father, lest not I be thine!
Tribunal terrible & pure, my God,
mercy for him and me.
Faces half-fanged, Christ drives abroad,
and though the crop hopes, Jane is so slipshod
I cry. Evil dissolves, & love, like foam;
that love. Prattle of children powers me home,
my heart claps like the swan's
under a frenzy of *who* love me & who shine.

As a canoe slides by on one strong stroke
hope his hélp not I, who do hardly bear
his gift still. But whisper
I am not utterly. I pare
an apple for my pipsqueak Mercy and
she runs & all need naked apples, fanned
their tinier envies.
Vomitings, trots, rashes. Can be hope a cloak?

for the man with cropt ears glares. My fingers tighten
my skirt. I pass. Alas! I pity all.
Shy, shy, with mé, Dorothy.
Moonrise, and frightening hoots. 'Mother,
how *long* will I be dead?' Our friend the owl
vanishes, darling, but your homing soul
retires on Heaven, Mercy:
not we one instant die, only our dark does lighten.

When by me in the dusk my child sits down
I am myself. Simon, if it's that loose,
let me wiggle it out.
You'll get a bigger one there, & bite.
How they loft, how their sizes delight and grate.
The proportioned, spiritless poems accumulate.
And they publish them
away in brutish London, for a hollow crown.

43

Father is not himself. He keeps his bed,
and threw a saffron scum Thursday. God-forsaken words
escaped him raving. Save,
Lord, thy servant zealous & just.
Sam he saw back from Harvard. He did scold
his secting enemies. His stomach is cold
while we drip, while
my baby John breaks out. O far from where he bred!

44

Bone of moaning: sung Where he has gone
a thousand summers by truth-hallowed souls;
be still. Agh, he is gone!
Where? I know. Beyond the shoal.
Still-all a Christian daughter grinds her teeth
a little. This our land has ghosted with
our dead: I am at home.
Finish, Lord, in me this work thou hast begun.

45

And they tower, whom the pear-tree lured
to let them fall, fierce mornings they reclined
down the brook-bank to the east
fishing for shiners with a crookt pin,
wading, dams massing, well, and Sam's to be
a doctor in Boston. After the divisive sea,
and death's first feast,
and the galled effort on the wilderness endured,

46

Arminians, and the King bore against us;
of an 'inward light' we hear with horror.
Whose fan is in his hand
and he will throughly purge his floor,
come towards mé. I have what licks the joints
and bites the heart, which winter more appoints.
Iller I, oftener.
Hard at the outset; in the ending thus hard, thus?

47

Sacred & unutterable Mind
flashing thorough the universe one thought,
I do wait without peace.
In the article of death I budge.
Eat my sore breath, Black Angel. Let me die.
Body a-drain, when will you be dry
and countenance my speed
to Heaven's springs? lest stricter writhings have me declined.

48

'What are those pictures in the air at night,
Mother?' Mercy did ask. Space charged with faces
day & night! I place
a goatskin's fetor, and sweat: fold me
in savoury arms. Something is shaking, wrong.
He smells the musket and lifts it. It is long.
It points at my heart.
Missed he must have. In the gross storm of sunlight

49

I sniff a fire burning without outlet,
consuming acrid its own smoke. It's me.
Ruined laughter sounds
outside. Ah but I waken, free.
And so I am about again. I hagged
a fury at the short maid, whom tongues tagged,
and I am sorry. Once
less I was anxious when more passioned to upset

50

the mansion & the garden & the beauty of God.
Insectile unreflective busyness
blunts & does amend.
Hangnails, piles, fibs, life's also.
But we are that from which draws back a thumb.
The seasons stream and, somehow, I am become
an old woman. It's so:
I look. I bear to look. Strokes once more his rod.

51

My window gives on the graves, in our great new house
(how many burned?) upstairs, among the elms.
I lie, & endure, & wonder.
A haze slips sometimes over my dreams
and holiness on horses' bells shall stand.
Wandering pacemaker, unsteadying friend,
in a redskin calm I wait:
beat when you will our end. Sinkings & droopings drowse.

52

They say thro' the fading winter Dorothy fails,
my second, who than I bore one more, nine;
and I see her inearthed. I linger.
Seaborn she wed knelt before Simon;
Simon I, and linger. Black-yellow seething, vast
it lies fróm me, mine: all they look aghast.
It will be a glorious arm.
Docile I watch. My wreckt chest hurts when Simon pales.

53

In the yellowing days your faces wholly fail,
at Fall's onset. Solemn voices fade.
I feel no coverlet.
Light notes leap, a beckon, swaying
the tilted, sickening ear within. I'll — I'll —
I am closed & coming. Somewhere! I defile
wide as a cloud, in a cloud,
unfit, desirous, glad — even the singings veil —

54

— You are not ready? You áre ready. Pass,
as shadow gathers shadow in the welling night.
Fireflies of childhood torch
you down. We commit our sister down.
One candle mourn by, which a lover gave,
the use's edge and order of her grave.
Quiet? Moisture shoots.
Hungry throngs collect. They sword into the carcass.

55

Headstones stagger under great draughts of time
after heads pass out, and their world must reel
speechless, blind in the end
about its chilling star: thrift tuft,
whin cushion — nothing. Already with the wounded flying
dark air fills, I am a closet of secrets dying,
races murder, foxholes hold men,
reactor piles wage slow upon the wet brain rime.

56

I must pretend to leave you. Only you draw off
a benevolent phantom. I say you seem to me
drowned towns off England,
featureless as those myriads
who what bequeathed save fire-ash, fossils, burled
in the open river-drifts of the Old World?
Simon lived on for years.
I renounce not even ragged glances, small teeth, nothing,

57

O all your ages at the mercy of my loves
together lie at once, forever or
so long as I happen.
In the rain of pain & departure, still
Love has no body and presides the sun,
and elfs from silence melody. I run.
Hover, utter, still,
a sourcing   whom my lost candle like the firefly loves.

Notes

Stanzas 1-4	The poem is about the woman, but this exordium is spoken by the poet, his voice modulating in stanza 4, line 8 [4.8] into hers.
1.1	He was not Governor until after her death.
1.5	Sylvester (the translator of Du Bartas) and Quarles, her favourite poets; unfortunately.
5.4,5	Many details are from quotations in Helen Campbell's biography, the Winthrop papers, narratives, town histories.
8.4ff.	Scriptural passages are sometimes ones she used herself, as this in her *Meditation liii*.
11.8	*that one*: the Old One.
12.5-13.2	The poet interrupts.
18.8	Her first child was not born until about 1633.
22.6	*chopping*: disputing, snapping, haggling; axing.
23.1	*fere*: his friend Death.
24.1	Her irony of 22.8 intensifies.
24.2	*rakes*: inclines, as a mast; bows.
25.3	One might say: He is enabled to speak, at last, in the fortune of a echo of her — and when she is loneliest (her former spiritual adviser having deserted Anne Hutchinson, and this her closest friend banished), as if she had summoned him; and only thus, perhaps, is she enabled to hear him. This second section of the poem is a dialogue, his voice however ceasing well before it ends at 39.4, and hers continuing for the whole third part, until the coda (54-57).
29.1-4	Cf. Isa. 1:5.
29.5,6	After a Klee.
33.1	Cf., on Byzantine icons, Frederick Rolfe ('Baron Corvo'): 'Who ever dreams of praying (with expecta-

tion of response) for the prayer of a Tintoretto or a Titian, or a Bellini, or a Botticelli? But who can refrain from crying "O Mother!" to these unruffleable wan dolls in indigo on gold?' (quoted from *The Desire and Pursuit of the Whole* by Graham Greene in *The Lost Childhood*).

33.5,6   'Délires des grandes profondeurs', described by Cousteau and others; a euphoria, sometimes fatal, in which the hallucinated diver offers passing fish his line, helmet, anything.

35.3,4   As of cliffhangers, movie serials wherein each week's episode ends with a train bearing down on the strapped heroine or with the hero dangling over an abyss into which Indians above him peer with satisfaction before they hatchet the rope.
          rescue: forcible recovery (by the owner) of goods distrained.

37.7,8   After an engraving somewhere in Fuchs's collections. *Bray*, above (36.4), puns.

39.5   The stanza is unsettled, like 24, by a middle line, signalling a broad transition.

42.8   *brutish*: her epithet for London in a kindly passage about the Great Fire.

46.1,2   Arminians, rebels against the doctrine of unconditional election. Her husband alone opposed the law condemning Quakers to death.

46.3,4   Matthew 3:12.

46.5,6   Rheumatic fever, after a celebrated French description.

48.2ff.   *Space . . . outside*: delirium.

51.5   Cf. Zech. 14:20.

51.6   *Wandering pacemaker*: a disease of the heart, here the heart itself.

52.4	Seaborn Cotton, John's eldest son; Bradstreet being then magistrate.
52.5,6	Dropsical, a complication of the last three years. Line 7 she actually said.
55.4	*thrift*: the plant, also called Our Lady's cushion.
55.8	*wet brain*: edema.
56.5,6	Cf. G. R. Levy, *The Gate of Horn*, p. 5.

EARLY POEMS

Winter Landscape

The three men coming down the winter hill
In brown, with tall poles and a pack of hounds
At heel, through the arrangement of the trees
Past the five figures at the burning straw,
Returning cold and silent to their town,

Returning to the drifted snow, the rink
Lively with children, to the older men,
The long companions they can never reach,
The blue light, men with ladders, by the church
The sledge and shadow in the twilit street,

Are not aware that in the sandy time
To come, the evil waste of history
Outstretched, they will be seen upon the brow
Of that same hill: when all their company
Will have been irrecoverably lost,

These men, this particular three in brown
Witnessed by birds will keep the scene and say
By their configuration with the trees,
The small bridge, the red houses and the fire,
What place, what time, what morning occasion

Sent them into the wood, a pack of hounds
At heel and the tall poles upon their shoulders,
Thence to return as now we see them and
Ankle-deep in snow down the winter hill
Descend, while three birds watch and the fourth flies.

The Statue

The statue, tolerant through years of weather,
Spares the untidy Sunday throng its look,
Spares shopgirls knowledge of the fatal pallor
Under their evening colour,
Spares homosexuals, the crippled, the alone,
Extravagant perception of their failure;
Looks only, cynical, across them all
To the delightful Avenue and its lights.

Where I sit, near the entrance to the Park,
The charming dangerous entrance to their need,
Dozens, a hundred men have lain till morning
And the preservative darkness waning,
Waking to want, to the day before, desire
For the ultimate good, Respect, to hunger waking;
Like the statue ruined but without its eyes;
Turned vaguely out at dawn for a new day.

Fountains I hear behind me on the left,
See green, see natural life springing in May
To spend its summer sheltering our lovers,
Those walks so shortly to be over.
The sound of water cannot startle them
Although their happiness runs out like water,
Of too much sweetness the expected drain.
They trust their Spring; they have not seen the statue.

Disfigurement is general. Nevertheless
Winters have not been able to alter its pride,
If that expression is a pride remaining,
Coriolanus and Rome burning,

An aristocracy that moves no more.
Scholars can stay their pity; from the ceiling
Watch blasted and superb inhabitants,
The sleepless justifying ruined stare.

Since graduating from its years of flesh
The name has faded in the public mind
Or doubled: which is this? the elder? younger?
The statesman or the traveller?
Who first died or who edited his works,
The lonely brother bound to remain longer
By a quarter-century than the first-born
Of that illustrious and lost family?

The lovers pass. Not one of them can know
Or care which Humboldt is immortalized.
If they glance up, they glance in passing,
An idle outcome of that pacing
That never stops, and proves them animal;
These thighs breasts pointed eyes are not their choosing,
But blind insignia by which are known
Season, excitement, loosed upon this city.

Turning: the brilliant Avenue, red, green,
The laws of passage; marvellous hotels;
Beyond, the dark apartment where one summer
Night an insignificant dreamer,
Defeated occupant, will close his eyes
Mercifully on the expensive drama
Wherein he wasted so much skill, such faith,
And salvaged less than the intolerable statue.

The Disciple

Summoned from offices and homes, we came.
By candle-light we heard him sing;
We saw him with a delicate length of string
Hide coins and lag a paper through a flame;
I was amazed by what that man could do.
And later on, in broad daylight,
He made someone sit suddenly upright
Who had lain long dead, whose face was blue.

But most he would astonish us with talk.
The warm sad cadence of his voice,
His compassion, our terror of his choice,
Brought each of us both glad and mad to walk
Beside him in the hills after sundown.
He spoke of birds, of children, long
And rubbing tribulation without song
For the indigent and crippled of this town.

Ventriloquist and strolling mage, from us,
Respectable citizens, he took
The hearts and swashed them in an upland brook,
Calling them his, all men's, anonymous.
. . He gained a certain notoriety;
The magical outcome of such love
The State saw it could not at all approve
And sought to learn where when that man would be.

The people he had entertained stood by,
I was among them, but one whom
He harboured kissed him for the coppers' doom,
Repenting later most most bitterly.

They ran him down and drove him up the hill.
He who had lifted but hearts stood
With thieves, performing still what tricks he could
For men to come, rapt in compassion still.

Great nonsense has been spoken of that time.
But I can tell you I saw then
A terrible darkness on the face of men,
His last astonishment; and now that I'm
Old I behold it as a young man yet.
None of us now knows what it means,
But to this day our loves and disciplines
Worry themselves there. We do not forget.

The Traveller

They pointed me out on the highway, and they said
'That man has a curious way of holding his head.'

They pointed me out on the beach; they said 'That man
Will never become as we are, try as he can.'

They pointed me out at the station, and the guard
Looked at me twice, thrice, thoughtfully & hard.

I took the same train that the others took,
To the same place. Were it not for that look
And those words, we were all of us the same.
I studied merely maps. I tried to name
The effects of motion on the travellers,
I watched the couple I could see, the curse
And blessings of that couple, their destination,
The deception practised on them at the station,
Their courage. When the train stopped and they knew
The end of their journey, I descended too.

The Spinning Heart

The fireflies and the stars our only light,
We rock, watching between the roses night
If we could see the roses. We cannot.
Where do the fireflies go by day, what eat?
What categories shall we use tonight?
The day was an exasperating day,
The day in history must hang its head
For the foul letters many women got,
Appointments missed, men dishevelled and sad
Before their mirrors trying to be proud.
But now (we say) the sweetness of the night
Will hide our imperfections from our sight,
For nothing can be angry or astray,
No man unpopular, lonely, or beset,
Where half a yellow moon hangs from a cloud.

Spinning however and balled up in space
All hearts, desires, pewter and honeysuckle,
What can be known of the individual face?
To the continual drum-beat of the blood
Mesh sea and mountain recollection, flame,
Motives in the corridor, touch by night,
Violent touch, and violence in rooms;
How shall we reconcile in any light
This blow and the relations that it wrecked?
Crescent the pressures on the singular act
Freeze it at last into its season, place,
Until the flood and disorder of Spring.
To Easterfield the court's best bore, defining
Space tied into a sailor's reef, our praise:
He too is useful, he is part of this,

Inimitable, tangible, post-human,
And Theo's disappointment has a place,
An item in that metamorphosis
The horrible coquetry of aging women.
Our superstitious barnacle our eyes
To the tide, the coming good; or has it come? —
Insufficient upon the beaches of the world
To drown that complex and that bestial drum.

Triumphant animal, — upon the rest
Bearing down hard, brooding, come to announce
The causes and directions of all this
Biting and breeding, — how will all your sons
Discover what you, assisted or alone,
Staring and sweating for seventy years,
Could never discover, the thing itself?
                              Your fears,
Fidelity, and dandelions grown
As big elephants, your morning lust
Can neither name nor control. No time for shame,
Whippoorwill calling, excrement falling, time
Rushes like a madman forward. Nothing can be known.

Parting as Descent

The sun rushed up the sky; the taxi flew;
There was a kind of fever on the clock
That morning. We arrived at Waterloo
With time to spare and couldn't find my track.

The bitter coffee in a small café
Gave us our conversation. When the train
Began to move, I saw you turn away
And vanish, and the vessels in my brain

Burst, the train roared, the other travellers
In flames leapt, burning on the tilted air
Che si cruccia, I heard the devils curse
And shriek with joy in that place beyond prayer.

Cloud and Flame

The summer cloud in summer blue
Capricious from the wind will run,
Laughing into the tender sun,
Knowing the work that it must do.
When One says liberty is vain
The cloud will come to summer rain.

After his college failure, Swift
Eight hours a day against his age
Began to document his rage
Towards the decades of strife and shift.
From claims that pride or party made
He kept in an exacting shade.

Cornford in a retreat was lost;
A stray shot like an aimless joke
His learning, spirit, at one stroke
Dispersed, his generation's cost.
The harvest value of his head
Is less than cloud, is less than bread.

The One recalls the many burn,
Prepared or unprepared: one flame
Within a shade can strike its name,
Another sees the cloud return.
And Thirkill saw the Christ's head shake
At Hastings, by the Bloody Lake.

Letter to His Brother

The night is on these hills, and some can sleep.
Some stare into the dark, some walk.
Only the sound of glasses and of talk,
Of cracking logs, imagining who weep,
Comes on the night wind to my waking ears.
Your enemies and mine are still,
None works upon us either good or ill:
Mint by the stream, tree-frogs, are travellers.

What shall I say for anniversary?
At Dachau yellow blows forbid
And Becket's brains upon his altar spread
Forbid my trust, or hungry prophecy.
Prediction if I make, I violate
The just expectancy of youth, —
Although you know as well as I whose tooth
Sunk in our heels, the western guise of fate.

When Patrick Barton chased the murderer
He heard behind him in the wood
Pursuit, and suddenly he knew hé fled:
He was the murderer, the others were
His vigilance. But when he crouched behind
A tree, the tree moved off and left
Him naked while the cry came on; he laughed
And like a hound he leapt out of his mind.

I wish for you — the moon was full, is gone —
Whatever bargain can be got
From the violent world our fathers bought,
For which we pay with fantasy at dawn,

Dismay at noon, fatigue, horror by night.
May love, or an image in work,
Bring you the brazen luck to sleep with dark
And so to get responsible delight.

1938

Desires of Men and Women

Exasperated, worn, you conjure a mansion,
The absolute butlers in the spacious hall,
Old silver, lace, and privacy, a house
Where nothing has for years been out of place,
Neither shoe-horn nor affection been out of place,
Breakfast in summer on the eastern terrace,
All justice and all grace.

                    At the reception
Most beautifully you conduct yourselves —
Expensive and accustomed, bow, speak French,
That Cinquecento miniature recall
The Duke presented to your great-grandmother —

And none of us, my dears, would dream of you
The half-lit and lascivious apartments
That are in fact your goal, for which you'd do
Murder if you had not your cowardice
To prop the law; or dream of you the rooms,
Glaring and inconceivably vulgar,
Where now you are, where now you wish for life,
Whence you project your naked fantasies.

World-Telegram

Man with a tail heads eastward for the Fair.
Can open a pack of cigarettes with it.
Was weaving baskets happily, it seems,
When found, the almost Missing Link, and brought
From Ceylon in the interests of science.
The correspondent doesn't know how old.

Two columns left, a mother saw her child
Crushed with its father by a ten-ton truck
Against a loading platform, while her son,
Small, frightened, in a Sea Scout uniform,
Watched from the Langley. All needed treatment.

Berlin and Rome are having difficulty
With a new military pact. Some think
Russia is not too friendly towards London.
The British note is called inadequate.

An Indian girl in Lima, not yet six,
Has been delivered by Caesarian.
A boy. They let the correspondent in:
Shy, uncommunicative, still quite pale,
A holy picture by her, a blue ribbon.

Right of the centre, and three columns wide,
A rather blurred but rather ominous
Machine-gun being set up by militia
This morning in Harlan County, Kentucky.
Apparently some miners died last night.
'Personal brawls' is the employers' phrase.

All this on the front page. Inside, penguins.
The approaching television of baseball.
The King approaching Quebec. Cotton down.
Skirts up. Four persons shot. Advertisements.
Twenty-six policemen are decorated.
Mother's Day repercussions. A film star
Hopes marriage will preserve him from his fans.

News of one day, one afternoon, one time.
If it were possible to take these things
Quite seriously, I believe they might
Curry disorders in the strongest brain,
Immobilize the most resilient will,
Stop trains, break up the city's food supply,
And perfectly demoralize the nation.

11 May 1939

Ancestor

The old men wept when the Old Man in blue
Bulked in the doorway of the train, Time spun
And in that instant's revolution Time
(Who cannot love old men) dealt carelessly
Passions and shames upon his hardihood,
Seeing the wet eyes of his former staff:

. . Crossing from Tennessee, the river at flood,
White River Valley, his original regiment,
The glowflies winking in the gully's dusk,
'Terrific & murderous' the Northern fire,
Three horses shot from under him at Shiloh
Fell, the first ball took Hindman's horse as well
And then the two legs from an orderly

Rain on the lost field, mire and violence,
Corruption; Klan-talk, a half-forgotten tongue
Rubbed up for By-Laws and its Constitution,
The Roman syllables
                              he an exile fled,
Both his plantations, great-grandmother's too
Gone, fled south and south into Honduras
Where great-grandmother was never reconciled
To monkeys or the thought of monkeys
                                                    once
Tricked into taking bites of one, she kept
Eight months her bed
                              fire on the colony,
Lifting of charges, and a late return,
The stranger in his land, and silence, silence

(Only the great grey riddled cloak spoke out
And sometimes a sudden breath or look spoke out)

Reflecting blue saw in the tears of men,
The tyrant shade, shade of the last of change,
And coughed once, twice, massive and motionless;
Now Federal, now Sheriff, near four-score,
Controlled with difficulty his old eyes
As he stepped down, for the first time, in blue.

The Animal Trainer (1)

I told him: The time has come, I must be gone.
It is time to leave the circus and circus days,
The admissions, the menagerie, the drums,
Excitements of disappointment and praise.
In a suburb of the spirit I shall seize
The steady and exalted light of the sun,
And live there, out of the tension that decays,
Until I become a man alone of noon.

Heart said: Can you do without your animals?
The looking, licking, smelling animals?
The friendly fumbling beast? The listening one?
That standing up and worst of animals?
What will become of you in the pure light
When all your enemies are gone, and gone
The inexhaustible prospect of the night?

— But the night is now the body of my fear,
These animals are my distraction. Once
Let me escape the smells and cages here,
Once let me stand naked in the sun,
All these performances will be forgotten.
I shall concentrate in the sunlight there.

Said the conservative Heart: Your animals
Are occupation, food for you, your love
And your immense responsibility;
They are the travellers by which you live.
(Without you they will pace and pine, or die.)

— I reared them, tended them (I said) and still
They plague me, they will not perform, they run
Into forbidden corners, they fight, they steal.
Better to live like an artist in the sun.

— You are an animal trainer, Heart replied.
Without your animals leaping at your side
No sun will save you, nor this bloodless pride.

— What must I do then? Must I stay and work
With animals, and confront the night, in the circus?

— You léarn from animals. You léarn in the dark.

The Animal Trainer (2)

I told him: The time has come, I must be gone.
It is time to leave the circus and circus days,
The admissions, the menagerie, the drums,
Excitements of disappointment and praise.
In a suburb of the spirit I shall seize
The steady and exalted light of the sun
And live there, out of the tension that decays,
Until I become a man alone of noon.

Heart said: Can you do without these animals?
The looking, licking, smelling animals?
The friendly fumbling beast? The listening one?
The standing up and worst of animals?
What will become of you in the pure light
When all your enemies are gone, and gone
The inexhaustible prospect of the night?

— But the night is now the body of my fear,
These animals are my distraction! Once
Let me escape the smells and cages here,
Once let me stand naked in the sun,
All their performances will be forgotten.
I shall concentrate in the sunlight there.

Said the conservative Heart: These animals
Are occupation, food for you, your love
And your despair, responsibility:
They are the travellers by which you live.
Without you they will pace and pine, or die.

— What soul-delighting tasks do they perform?
They quarrel, snort, leap, lie down, their delight
Merely a punctual meal and to be warm.
Justify their existence in the night!

— The animals are coupling, and they cry
'The circus *is*, it is our mystery,
It is a world of dark where animals die.'

— Animals little and large, be still, be still:
I'll stay with you. Suburb and sun are pale.

— Animals are your destruction, and your will.

1 September 1939

The first, scattering rain on the Polish cities.
That afternoon a man squat' on the shore
Tearing a square of shining cellophane.
Some easily, some in evident torment tore,
Some for a time resisted, and then burst.
All this depended on fidelity . .
One was blown out and borne off by the waters,
The man was tortured by the sound of rain.

Children were sent from London in the morning
But not the sound of children reached his ear.
He found a mangled feather by the lake,
Lost in the destructive sand this year
Like feathery independence, hope. His shadow
Lay on the sand before him, under the lake
As under the ruined library our learning.
The children play in the waves until they break.

The Bear crept under the Eagle's wing and lay
Snarling; the other animals showed fear,
Europe darkened its cities. The man wept,
Considering the light which had been there,
The feathered gull against the twilight flying.
As the little waves ate away the shore
The cellophane, dismembered, blew away.
The animals ran, the Eagle soared and dropt.

Desire is a World by Night

The history of strangers in their dreams
Being irresponsible, is fun for men,
Whose sons are neither at the Front nor frame
Humiliating weakness to keep at home
Nor wtnce on principle, wearing mother grey,
Honoured by radicals. When the mind is free
The catechetical mind can mincn and tear
Contemptible vermin from a stranger's hair
And then sleep.

　　　　　　　In our parents' dreams we see
Vigour abutting on senility,
Stiff blood, and weathered with the years, poor vane;
Unfortunate but inescapable.
Although this wind bullies the windowpane
Are the children to be kept responsible
For the world's decay? Carefully we choose
Our fathers, carefully we cut out those
On whom to exert the politics of praise.

Heard after dinner, in defenceless ease,
The dreams of friends can puzzle, dazzle us
With endless journeys through unfriendly snow,
Malevolent faces that appear and frown
Where nothing was expected, the sudden stain
On spotless window-ledges; these we take
Chuckling, but take them with us when we go,
To study in secret, late, brooding, looking
For trails and parallels. We have a stake
In this particular region, and we look
Excitedly for situations that we know.

— The disinterested man has gone abroad;
Winter is on the by-way where he rode
Erect and alone, summery years ago.

When we dream, paraphrase, analysis
Exhaust the crannies of the night. We stare,
Fresh sweat upon our foreheads, as they fade:
The melancholy and terror of avenues
Where long no single man has moved, but play
Under the arc-lights gangs of the grey dead
Running directionless. That bright blank place
Advances with us into fearful day,
Heady and insuppressible. Call in friends,
They grin and carry it carefully away, —
The fathers can't be trusted, — strangers wear
Their strengths, and visor. Last, authority,
The Listener borrow from an English grave
To solve our hatred and our bitterness . .
The foul and absurd to solace or dismay.
All this will never appear; we will not say;
Let the evidence be buried in a cave
Off the main road. If anyone could see
The white scalp of that passionate will and those
Sullen desires, he would stumble, dumb,
Retreat into the time from which he came
Counting upon his fingers and his toes.

The Moon and the Night and the Men

On the night of the Belgian surrender the moon rose
Late, a delayed moon, and a violent moon
For the English or the American beholder;
The French beholder. It was a cold night,
People put on their wraps, the troops were cold
No doubt, despite the calendar, no doubt
Numbers of refugees coughed, and the sight
Or sound of some killed others. A cold night.

On Outer Drive there was an accident:
A stupid well-intentioned man turned sharp
Right and abruptly he became an angel
Fingering an unfamiliar harp,
Or screamed in hell, or was nothing at all.
Do not imagine this is unimportant.
He was a part of the night, part of the land,
Part of the bitter and exhausted ground
Out of which memory grows.

                    Michael and I
Stared at each other over chess, and spoke
As little as possible, and drank and played.
The chessmen caught in the European eye,
Neither of us I think had a free look
Although the game was fair. The move one made
It was difficult at last to keep one's mind on.
'. . hurt and unhappy' said the man in London.
We said to each other, The time is coming near
When none shall have books or music, none his dear,
And only a fool will speak aloud his mind.
History is approaching a speechless end,
As Henry Adams said. Adams was right.

All this occurred on the night when Leopold
Fulfilled the treachery four years before
Begun — or was he well-intentioned, more
Roadmaker to hell than king? At any rate,
The moon came up late and the night was cold,
Many men died — although we know the fate
Of none, nor of anyone, and the war
Goes on, and the moon in the breast of man is cold.

LATER POEMS

The Ball Poem

What is the boy now, who has lost his ball,
What, what is he to do? I saw it go
Merrily bouncing, down the street, and then
Merrily over — there it is in the water!
No use to say 'O there are other balls':
An ultimate shaking grief fixes the boy
As he stands rigid, trembling, staring down
All his young days into the harbour where
His ball went. I would not intrude on him,
A dime, another ball, is worthless. Now
He senses first responsibility
In a world of possessions. People will take balls,
Balls will be lost always, little boy,
And no one buys a ball back. Money is external.
He is learning, well behind his desperate eyes,
The epistemology of loss, how to stand up
Knowing what every man must one day know
And most know many days, how to stand up.
And gradually light returns to the street,
A whistle blows, the ball is out of sight,
Soon part of me will explore the deep and dark
Floor of the harbour . . I am everywhere,
I suffer and move, my mind and my heart move
With all that move me, under the water
Or whistling, I am not a little boy.

Canto Amor

Dream in a dream the heavy soul somewhere
struck suddenly & dark down to its knees.
A griffin sighs off in the orphic air.

If (Unknown Majesty) I not confess
praise for the wrack the rock the live sailor
under the blue sea, — yet I may You bless

always for hér, in fear & joy for hér
whose gesture summons ever when I grieve
me back and is my mage and minister.

— Muses: whose worship I may never leave
but for this pensive woman, now I dare,
teach me her praise! with her my praise receive. —

Three years already of the round world's war
had rolled by stoned & disappointed eyes
when she and I came where we were made for.

Pale as a star lost in returning skies,
more beautiful than midnight stars more frail
she moved towards me like chords, a sacrifice;

entombed in body trembling through the veil
arm upon arm, learning our ancient wound,
we see our one soul heal, recovering pale.

Then priestly sanction, then the drop of sound.
Quickly part to the cavern ever warm
deep from the march, body to body bound,

descend (my soul) out of dismantling storm
into the darkness where the world is made.
. . Come back to the bright air. Love is multiform.

Heartmating hesitating unafraid
although incredulous, she seemed to fill
the lilac shadow with light wherein she played,

whom sorry childhood had made sit quite still,
an orphan silence, unregarded sheen,
listening for any small soft note, not hopeful:

caricature: as once a maiden Queen,
flowering power comeliness kindness grace,
shattered her mirror, wept, would not be seen.

These pities moved. Also above her face
serious or flushed, swayed her fire-gold
not earthly hair, now moonless to unlace,

resistless flame, now in a sun more cold
great shells to whorl about each secret ear,
mysterious histories, white shores, unfold.

New musics! One the music that we hear,
this is the music which the masters make
out of their minds, profound solemn & clear.

And then the other music, in whose sake
all men perceive a gladness but we are drawn
less for that joy than utterly to take

our trial, naked in the music's vision,
the flowing ceremony of trouble and light,
all Loves becoming, none to flag upon.

Such Mozart made, — an ear so delicate
he fainted at a trumpet-call, a child
so delicate. So merciful that sight,

so stern, we follow rapt, who ran a-wild.
Marriage is the second music, and thereof
we hear what we can bear, faithful & mild.

Therefore the streaming torches in the grove
through dark or bright, swiftly & now more near
cherish a festival of anxious love.

Dance for this music, Mistress to music dear,
more, that storm worries the disordered wood
grieving the midnight of my thirtieth year

and only the trial of our music should
still this irresolute air, only your voice
spelling the tempest may compel our good:

Sigh then beyond my song: whirl & rejoice!

The Enemies of the Angels

I

The Irish and the Italians own the place.
Anyone owns it, if you like, who has
A dollar minimum; but it is theirs by noise.
Let them possess it until one o'clock,
The balconies' tiers, huddled tables, shroud-
ed baleful music, and the widening crack
Across the far wall watching a doomed crowd,
The fat girl simpering carnations to the boys.

This is a paradise the people seek,
To hide, if they but knew, being awake,
Losses and crisis. This is where they come
For love, for fun, to forget, dance, to conceal
Their slow perplexity by the river. Who
But pities the kissing couple? Who would feel
Disdain, as she does, being put on show
By whom she loves? And pity . . our images of home.

The arrival of the angels is delayed
An even minute, and I am afraid
We clapped because they fail to, not because
They come. Their wings are sorry. The platform
A little shudders as they back and frisk,
We'd maul the angels, the whole room is warm, —
A waste, and a creation without risk;
Jostling, pale as they vanish, the horse-faced chorine
    paws.

The impersonator is our special joy
And puzzle: did the nurse announce a boy
Or not? But now the guy is all things, all
Women and most men howl when he takes off
Our President, the Shadow, Garbo or Bing
And other marvellous persons. 'Sister Rough'
The sailors at their table, gesturing,
Soprano, whistling. Still, recall him, and recall

Mimics we wish we all were, and we are.
We lack a subject just, we lack a car,
We would see two Mayors bowing as we pass,
We wish we had another suit, we wish
Another chance, we would have Western life
Where the hero reins and fans, horseflesh is flesh.
But the heckling man and his embarrassed wife
Play us across the mirrored room. Where is my glass?

II

My tall and singular friend two feet away,
Where do you go at the end of another day?
What is your lot, your wife's lot, under the Lord?
If you between two certain ages, more
Nor less, are, and if you revere the Flag
Or whether, Friend, you find a flag a bore
And whether Democracy blooms or you see it sag,
What is your order number at your Local Board?

Where do you all go? Not with whom you would;
But where you went as little boys, when good,
To the plains' heaven of the silver screen.
This comic in a greatcoat is your will,

The faery presence walking among men
Who mock him: sly, baffled, and powerful
For imagination is his, and imagination
Ruins, compels; consider the comedian again.

The orchestra returns and tunes before
A spot, a flash, the M.C. through the door
Glides like a breakfast to your vision — gay
Indelicate intimate, 'Jerk, what do you know?'
An aging, brimstone acrobat in pink
Monkeys her way across the blue boards. Who
Resists her? Who would be unkind to think
A human wheel, a frozen smile, is human woe?

Consider, students, at the convalescent hour
The fantasy which last week you saw fair,
Which loses now its eye; its eye is gone.
Where shall the ten be found to safe us? For
The enemies of the angels, hard on sleep,
Weary themselves to find the Gentleman's door.
It is not a little one. Perhaps you weep,
Three eyes weep in the world you inhabit alone.

All this resist. Who wish their stays away
Or wish them tighter tighter — the mourners pray
In narrowing circles — these are women lost,
Are men lost in the drag of women's eyes,
Salt mouths. Go with the tide, at midnight dream
Hecklers will vanish like a radical's lies,
And all Life slides from drink to drink, the stream
Slides, and under the stream we join a happy ghost.

Boston Common

1

Slumped under the impressive genitals
Of the bronze charger, protected by bronze,
By darkness from patrols, by sleep from what
Assailed him earlier and left him here,
The man lies. Clothing and organs. These were once
Shoes. Faint in the orange light
Flooding the portico above: the whole
Front of the State House. On a February night.

2

Dramatic bivouac for the casual man!
Beyond the exedra the Common falls,
Famous and dark, away; a lashing wind;
Immortal heroes in a marble frame
Who broke their bodies on Fort Wagner's walls,
Robert Gould Shaw astride, and his
Negroes without name, who followed, who fell
Screaming or calm, wet cold, sick or oblivious.

3

Who now cares how? here they are in their prime, —
Paradigm, pitching imagination where
The crucible night all singularity,
Idiosyncrasy and creed, burnt out
And brought them, here, a common character.
Imperishable march below
The mounted man below the Angel, and
Under, the casual man, the possible hero.

4

Hero for whom under a sky of bronze,
Saint-Gaudens' sky? Passive he seems to lie,
The last straw of contemporary thought,
In shapeless failure; but may be this man
Before he came here, or he comes to die,
Blazing with force or fortitude
Superb of civil soul may stand or may
After young Shaw within that crucible have stood.

5

For past her assignation when night fell
And the men forward, — poise and shock of dusk
As daylight rocking passes the horizon, —
The Angel spread her wings still. War is the
Congress of adolescents, love in a mask,
Bestial and easy, issueless,
Or gets a man of bronze. No beating heart
Until the casual man can see the Angel's face.

6

Where shall they meet? what ceremony find,
Loose in the brothel of another war
This winter night? Can citizen enact
His timid will and expectation where,
Exact a wedding or her face O where
Tanks and guns, tanks and guns,
Move and must move to their conclusions, where
The will is mounted and gregarious and bronze?

7

For ceremony, in the West, in the East,
The pierced sky, iced air, and the rent of cloud
As, moving to his task at dawn, who'd been
Hobbledehoy of the cafeteria life
Swung like a hobby in the blue and rode
The shining body of his choice
To the eye and time of his bombardier; —
Stiffened in the racket, and relaxed beyond noise.

8

'Who now cares how?' — the quick, the index! Question
Your official heroes in a magazine,
Wry voices past the river. Dereliction,
Lust and bloodlust, error and goodwill, this one
Died howling, craven, this one was a swine
From childhood. Man and animal
Sit for their photographs to Fame, and dream
Barbershop hours . . vain, compassionate parable.

9

'Accidents of history, memorials' —
A considering and quiet voice. 'I see
Photograph and bronze upon another shore
Do not arrive; the light is where it is,
Indifferent to honour. Let honour be
Consolation to those who give,
None to the Hero, and no sign of him:
All unrecorded, flame-like, perish and live.'

10

Diminishing beyond the elms. Rise now
The chivalry and defenders of our time,
From Spain and China, the tortured continents,
Leningrad, Syria, Corregidor, —
Upon a primitive theme high variations
Like Beethoven's. — Lost, lost!
Whose eyes hung faultless to one horizon
Their fan look. Fiery night consumes a summoned ghost.

11

Images of the Possible, the top,
Their time they taxed, — after the tanks came through,
When orderless and by their burning homes'
Indelible light, with knee and nail they struck
(The improvised the real) man's common foe,
Misled blood-red statistical men.
Images of conduct in a crucible,
Their eyes, and nameless eyes, which will not come again.

12

We hope will not again. Therefore those eyes
Fix me again upon the terrible shape,
Defeated and marvellous, of the man I know,
Jack under the stallion. We have passed him by,
Wandering, prone, and he is our whole hope,
Our fork's one tine and our despair,
The heart of the Future beating. How far far
We sent our subtle messengers! when he is here.

13

Who chides our clamour and who would forget
The death of heroes: never know the shore
Where, hair to the West, Starkatterus was burnt;
And undergo no more that spectacle —
Perpetually verdant the last pyre,
Fir, cypress, yew, the phoenix bay
And voluntary music — which to him
Threw never meat or truth. He looks another way,

14

Watching who labour O that all may see
And savour the blooming world, flower and sound,
Tending and tending to peace, — be what their blood,
Prayer, occupation may — so tend for all:
A common garden in a private ground.
Who labour in the private dark
And silent dark for birthday music and light,
Fishermen, gardeners, about their violent work.

15

Lincoln, the lanky lonely and sad man
Who suffered in Washington his own, his soul;
Mao Tse-Tung, Teng Fa, fabulous men,
Laughing and serious men; or Tracy Doll
Tracing the future on the wall of a cell —
There, there, on the wall of a cell
The face towards which we hope all history,
Institutions, tears move, there the Individual.

16

Ah, it may not be so. Still the crucial night
Fastens you all upon this frame of hope:
Each in his limited sick world with them,
The figures of his reverence, his awe,
His shivering devotion, — that they shape
Shelter, action, salvation.
. . Legends and lies. Kneel if you will, but rise
Homeless, alone, and be the kicking working one.

17

None anywhere alone! The turning world
Brings unaware us to our enemies,
Artist to assassin, Saint-Gaudens' bronze
To a free shelter, images to end.
The cold and hard wind has tears in my eyes,
Long since, long since, I heard the last
Traffic unmeshing upon Boylston Street,
I halted here in the orange light of the Past,

18

Helpless under the great crotch lay this man
Huddled against woe, I had heard defeat
All day, I saw upon the sands assault,
I heard the voice of William James, the wind,
And poured in darkness or in my heartbeat
Across my hearing and my sight
Worship and love irreconcilable
Here to be reconciled. On a February night.

1942

Young Woman's Song

The round and smooth, my body in my bath,
If someone else would like it too. — I did,
I wanted T. to think 'How interesting'
Although I hate his voice and face, hate both.
I hate this something like a bobbing cork
Not going. I want something to hang to. —

A free wind roaring high up in the bare
Branches of trees, — I suppose it was lust
But it was holy and awful. All day I thought
I am a bobbing cork, irresponsible child
Loose on the waters. — What have you done at last?
A little work, a little vague chat.

I want that £3.10 hat terribly. —
What I am looking for (*I am*) may be
Happening in the gaps of what I know.
The full moon does go with you as yóu go.
Where am I going? I am not afraid . .
Only I would be lifted lost in the flood.

The Song of the Demented Priest

I put those things there. — See them burn.
The emerald the azure and the gold
Hiss and crack, the blues & greens of the world
As if I were tired. Someone interferes
Everywhere with me. The clouds, the clouds are torn
In ways I do not understand or love.

Licking my long lips, I looked upon God
And he flamed and he was friendlier
Than you were, and he was small. Showing me
Serpents and thin flowers; these were cold.
Dominion waved & glittered like the flare
From ice under a small sun. I wonder.

Afterward the violent and formal dancers
Came out, shaking their pithless heads.
I would instruct them but I cannot now, —
Because of the elements. They rise and move,
I nod a dance and they dance in the rain
In my red coat. I am the king of the dead.

The Song of the Young Hawaiian

Ai, they all pass in front of me those girls!
Blazing and lazy colours. A swaying sun
Brushes the brown tips of them stiffly softly
And whispers me: Never take only one
As the yellow men the white the foreigners do. —
No no, I dance them all.

The old men come to me at dusk and say
'Hang from their perches now the ruined birds;
They will fall. We hear strange languages.
Rarely a child sings now.' They cough and say
'We are a dying race.' Ai! if we are!
You will not marry me.

Strengthless the tame will of the elders' eyes. —
The green palms, the midnight sand, the creaming surf!
The sand at streaming noon is black. I swim
Farther than others, for I swim alone.
. . (Whom Nangganangga smashed to pieces on
The road to Paradise.)

A Professor's Song

(. . rabid or dog-dull.) Let me tell you how
The Eighteenth Century couplet ended. Now
Tell me. Troll me the sources of that Song —
Assigned last week — by Blake. Come, come along,
Gentlemen. (Fidget and huddle, do. Squint soon.)
I want to end these fellows all by noon.

'That deep romantic chasm' — an early use;
The word is from the French, by our abuse
Fished out a bit. (Red all your eyes. O when?)
'A poet is a man speaking to men':
But I am then a poet, am I not? —
Ha ha. The radiator, please. Well, what?

Alive now — no — Blake would have written prose,
But movement following movement crisply flows,
So much the better, better the much so,
As burbleth Mozart. Twelve. The class can go.
Until I meet you, then, in Upper Hell
Convulsed, foaming immortal blood: farewell.

The Captain's Song

The tree before my eyes bloomed into flame,
I rode the flame. This was the element,
Forsaking wife and child, I came to find, —
The flight through arrowy air dark as a dream
Brightening and falling, the loose tongues blue
Like blood above me, until I forgot.

. . Later, forgetting, I became a child
And fell down without reason and played games
Running, being the fastest, before dark
And often cried. Certain things I hid
That I had never liked, I leapt the stream
No one else could and spurted off alone . .

You crippled Powers, cluster to me now:
Baffle this memory from my return,
That in the coldest nights, murmuring her name
I sought her two feet with my feet, my feet
Were warm and hers were ice and I warmed her
With both of mine. Will I warm her with one?

The Song of the Tortured Girl

After a little I could not have told —
But no one asked me this — why I was there.
I asked. The ceiling of that place was high
And there were sudden noises, which I made.
I must have stayed there a long time today:
My cup of soup was gone when they brought me back.

Often 'Nothing worse now can come to us'
I thought, the winter the young men stayed away,
My uncle died, and mother cracked her crutch.
And then the strange room where the brightest light
Does not shine on the strange men: shines on me.
I feel them stretch my youth and throw a switch.

Through leafless branches the sweet wind blows
Making a mild sound, softer than a moan;
High in a pass once where we put our tent,
Minutes I lay awake to hear my joy.
— I no longer remember what they want. —
Minutes I lay awake to hear my joy.

The Song of the Bridegroom

A sort of anxiousness crystal in crystal has . .
Fragile and open like these pairs of eyes.
All over all things move to stare at it.
One's single wish now: to be laid away
Felted in depths of caves, dark cupboards that
No one would open for a long time. —

Do not approach me! If I am on show
Compassion waves you past, you hoverers,
Forms brutal, beating eyes upon my window,
Because if I am desolate I have —
Have emanations, and it is not safe.
Rising and falling fire, ceremonial fire.

Not long . . not long but like a journey home
Frightening after so distant years
And such despairs . . And then fatigue sets in.
Lead me up blindly now where I began,
I will not wince away into my one.
I extend my hand and place it in the womb.

Song of the Man Forsaken and Obsessed

Viridian and gamboge and vermilion
Are and are not. — The hut is quiet,
Indistinct as letters. When I wake I wait.
Nothing comes. — The brown girl brings me rice
And one day months ago I might have stood —
So far were firm my feet — had that ship come —
And painted, softening my brush with blood.

Hardly, whatever happens from today.
— Certainly the little old woman
With a white eye, who takes all things away,
Comes and stares from the corner of my bed
If I could turn. My nails and my hair loosen,
The stiff flesh lurches and flows off like blood.

Grateful the surf of death drawing back under
(Offshore to fan out, vague and dark again)
My legs, my decayed feet, cock and heart.
If I were rid of them, somehow propped up . .
My bloody brain alone with a little vermilion!

The Pacifist's Song

I am the same yes as you others, only —
(Also for mé the plain where I was born,
Bore Her look, bear love, makes its mindless pull
And matters in my throat, also for me
The many-murdered sway my dreams unshorn,
Bearded with woe, their eyes blasted and dull)

Only I wake out of the vision of death
And hear One whisper whether man or god
'Kill not . . Your ill from evil comes . . Bear all'; —
Only I must forsake my country's wrath
Who am earth's citizen, must human blood
Anywhere shed mourn, turning from it pale

Back to the old and serious labour, to
My restless labour under the vigilant stars,
From whom no broad storm ever long me hides.
What I try, doomed, is hard enough to do.
We breed up in our own breast our worse wars
Who long since sealed ourselves Hers Who abides.

Surviving Love

The clapper hovers, but why run so hard?
What he wants, has, — more than will make him ease;
No god calls down, — he's not been on his knees
This man, for years, and he is off his guard.
What then does he dream of
Sweating through day? — Surviving love.

Cold he knows he comes, once to the dark,
All that waste of cold, leaving all cold
Behind him hearts, forgotten when he's tolled,
His books are split and sold, the pencil mark
He made erased, his wife
Gone brave & quick to her new life.

And so he spins to find out something warm
To think on when the glaze fastens his eyes
And he begins to freeze. He slows and tries
To hear a promise: 'After, after your storm
I will grieve and remember,
Miss you and be warm and remember.'

But really nothing replies to the poor man,
He never hears this, or the voice he hears
(He thinks) he loses ah when next appears
The hood of the bell, seeing which he began.
His skull rings with his end,
He runs on, love for love.

The Lightning

Sick with the lightning lay my sister-in-law,
Concealing it from her children, when I came.
What I could, did, helpless with what I saw.

Analysands all, and the rest ought to be,
The friends my innocence cherished, and you and I,
Darling, — the friends I qualm and cherish and see.

. . The fattest nation! — wé do not thrive fat
But facile in the scale with all we rise
And shift a breakfast, and there is shame in that.

And labour sweats with vice at the top, and two
Bullies are bristling. What he thought who thinks?
It is difficult to say what one will do.

Obstinate, gleams from the black world the gay and fair,
My love loves choclate, she loves also me,
And the lightning dances, but I cannot despair.

Fare Well

Motions of waking trouble winter air,
I wonder, and his face as it were forms
Solemn, canorous, under the howled alarms, —
The eyes shadowed and shut.
Certainly for this sort of thing it is very late,
I shudder, while my love longs and I pour
My bright eyes towards the moving shadow .. where?
Out, like a plucked gut.

What has been taken away will not return,
I take it, whether upon the crouch of night
Or for my mountain need to share a morning's light, —
No! I am alone.
What has been taken away should not have been shown,
I complain, torturing, and then withdrawn.
After so long, can I still long so and burn,
Imperishable son?

O easy the phoenix in the tree of the heart,
Each in its time, his twigs and spices fixes
To make a last nest, and marvellously relaxes, —
Out of the fire, weak peep! ..
Father I fought for Mother, sleep where you sleep!
I slip into a snowbed with no hurt
Where warm will warm be warm enough to part
Us. As I sink, I weep.

Rock-study with Wanderer

'Cold cold cold of a special night'
Summer and winter sings under the beast
The ravished doll   Hear in the middle waste
The blue doll of the west cracking with fright

The music & the lights did not go out
Alas   Our foreign officers are gay
Singers in the faery cities shiver & play
Their exile dances through unrationed thought

Waiting for the beginning of the end
The wedding of the arms   Whose charnel arms
Will plough the emerald mathematical farms
In spring, spring-flowers to the U.N. send?

*   *   *

Waiting I stroll within a summer wood
Avoiding broken glass in the slant sun
Our promises we may at last make good
The stained glass shies when the cathedral's won

Certainly in a few years call it peace
The arms & wings of peace patrol us all
The planes & arms that planes & arms may cease
Pathos (theanthropos) fills evenfall

When shall the body of the State come near
The body's state stable & labile? When
Irriding & resisting rage & fear
Shall men in unison yet resemble men?

Detroit our heart   When terribly we move
The sea is ours   We walk upon the sea
The air is ours   Hegemony, my love,
The good life's founded upon LST

The twilight birds wake   A paralysis
Is busy with societies and souls
Whose gnarled & pain-wild bodies beg abyss
Paraplegia dolorosa   The world rolls

A tired and old man resting on the grass
His forehead loose, as if he had put away
Among the sun & the green & the young who pass
The whole long fever of his passionate day

. . To the dark watcher then an hour comes
Neither past nor future, when the chuffing sea
Far off like the rough of beast nearby succumbs
And a kind of sleep spreads over rock & tree

Nightshade not far from the abandoned tomb
Hangs its still bells & fatal berries down
The flowers dream   Crags shadows loom
The caresses of the animals are done

Under faint moon they lie absorbed and fair
Stricken their limbs flow in false attitudes
Of love   Dovetailed into a broken mirror
Stained famous glass are, where the watcher broods

All wars are civil   So the thing will die
Your civilization a glitter of great glass
The lusts have shivered you are shaken by
To step aside from in the moonlit grass

Stare on, cold riot of the western mind
Rockwalking man, what can a wanderer know?
Rattle departing of his friend and kind
And then (the widow sang) sphincter let go

*   *   *

Draw, draw the curtain on a little life
A filth a fairing   Wood is darkening
Where birdcall hovered now I hear no thing
I hours since came from my love my wife

Although a strange voice sometimes patiently
Near in the air when I lie vague and weak
As if it had a body tries to speak . .
I must go back, she will be missing me

Whether There Is Sorrow in the Demons

Near the top a bad turn some dare. Well,
The horse swerves and screams, his eyes pop,
Feet feel air, the firm winds prop
Jaws wide wider until
Through great teeth rider greets the smiles of Hell.

Thick night, where the host's thews crack like thongs
A welcome, curving abrupt on cheek & neck.
No wing swings over once to check
Lick of their fire's tongues,
Whip & chuckle, hoarse insulting songs.

Powers immortal, fixed, intractable.
Only the lost soul jerks whom they joy hang:
Clap of remorse, and tang and fang
More frightful than the drill
An outsize dentist scatters down a skull;

Nostalgia rips him swinging. Fast in malice
How may his masters mourn, how ever yearn
The frore pride wherein they burn?
God's fire. To what *qui tollis*
Stone-tufted ears prick back towards the bright Palace?

Whence Lucifer shone Lucifer's friends hail
The scourge of choice made at the point of light
Destined into eternal night;
Motionless to fulfil
Their least, their envy looks up dense and pale.

. . Repine blackmarket felons; murderers
Sit still their time, till yellow feet go first,
Dies soon in them, and can die, thirst;
Not lives in these, nor years
On years scar their despair — which yet rehearse . .

Their belvedere is black. They believe, and quail.
One shudder racks them only, lonely, and
No mirror cracks at their command.
Unsocketed, their will
Grinds on their fate. So was, so shall be still.

The Long Home

bulks where the barley blew, time out of mind
Of the sleepless Master. The barbered lawn
Far to a grey wall lounges, the birds are still,
Rising wind rucks from the sill
The slack brocade beside the old throne he dreams on.
The portraits' hands are blind.

Below these frames they strain on stone. He mumbles . .
Fathers who listen, what loves hear
Surfacing from the lightless past? He foams.
Stillness locks a hundred rooms.
Louts in a bar aloud, The People, sucking beer.
A barefoot kiss. Who trembles?

Peach-bloom, sorb-apple sucked in what fine year!
I am a wine, he wonders; when?
Am I what I can do? My large white hands.
Boater & ascot, in grandstands
Coups. Concentrations of frightful cold, and then
Warm limbs below a pier.

The Master is sipping his identity.
Ardours & stars! Trash humped on trash.
The incorporated yacht, the campaign cheque
Signed one fall on the foredeck
Hard on a quarrel, to   amaze the fool. Who brash
Hectored out some false plea?

Brownpaper-blind, his morning passions trailed
Home in the clumsy dusk, — how now
Care which from which, trapped on a racing star

Where we know not who we are! . .
The whipcord frenzy curls, he slouches where his brow
Works like the rivals' failed.

Of six young men he flew to breakfast as,
Only the magpie, rapist, stayed
For dinner, and the rapist died, so that
Not the magpie but the cat
Vigil upon the magpie stalks, sulky parade,
Great tail switching like jazz.

Frightened, dying to fly, pied and obscene,
He blinks his own fantastic watch
For the indolent Spring of what he was before;
A stipple of sunlight, clouded o'er,
Remorse a scribble on   the magic tablet which
A schoolboy thumb jerks clean.

Heat lightning straddles the horizon dusk
Above the yews: the fresh wind blows:
He flicks a station on by the throne-side . .
Out in the wide world, Kitty — wide
Night — *far across the sea* . . Some guardian accent grows
Below the soft voice, brusque:

'You are: not what you wished but what you were,
The decades' vise your gavel brands,
You glare the god who gobbled his own fruit,
He who stood mute, lucid and mute,
Under peine forte et dure to will his bloody lands,
Then whirled down without heir.'

The end of which he will not know. Undried,
A prune-skin helpless on his roof.
His skin gleams in the lamplight dull as gold
And old gold clusters like mould
Stifling about his blood, time's helm to build him proof.
Thump the oak, and preside!

An ingrown terrible smile unflowers, a sigh
Blurs, the axle turns, unmanned.
Habited now forever with his weight
Well-housed, he rolls in the twilight
Unrecognizable   against the world's rim, and
A bird whistles nearby.

Whisked off, a voice, fainter, faint, a guise,
A gleam, pin of a, a. Nothing.
— One look round last, like rats, before we leave.
A famous house. Now the men arrive:
Horror, they swing their cold   bright mallets, they're
       breaking
Him up before my eyes!

Wicked vistas! The wolves mourn for our crime
Out past the grey wall. On to our home,
Whereby the barley may seed and resume.
Mutter of thrust stones palls this room,
The crash of mallets. He   is going where I come,
Barefoot soul fringed with rime.

A Winter-piece to a Friend Away

Your letter came. — Glutted the earth & cold
With rains long heavy, follows intense frost;
    Snow howls and hides the world
We workt awhile to build; all the roads are lost;
Icy spiculae float, filling strange air;
No voice goes far; one is alone whirling since where,
    And when was it one crossed?
    You have been there.

I too the breaking blizzard's eddies bore
One year, another year; tempted to drop
    At my own feet forlorn
Under the warm fall, frantic more to chop
Wide with the gale until my thought ran numb
Clenching the blue skin tight against what white
      spikes come,
    And the sick brain estop.
    Your pendulum

Mine, not stilled wholly, has been sorry for,
Weeps from, and would instruct . . Unless I lied
    What word steadies that cord?
Glade grove & ghyll of antique childhood glide
Off; from our grown grief, weathers that appal,
The massive sorrow of the mental hospital,
    Friends & our good friends hide.
    They came to call.

Hardly theirs, moment when the tempest gains,
Loose heart convulses. Their hearts bend off dry,
     Their fruit dangles and fades.
— Solicitudes of the orchard heart, comply
A little with my longing, a little sing
Our sorrow among steel & glass, our stiffening,
     That hers may modify:
     O trembling Spring. —

Immortal risks our sort run, to a house
Reported in a wood . . mould upon bread
     And brain, breath giving out,
From farms we go by, barking, and shaken head,
The shrunk pears hang, Hölderlin's weathercock
Rattles to tireless wind, the fireless landscape rock,
     Artists insane and dead
     Strike like a clock:

If the fruit is dead, fast. Wait. Chafe your left wrist.
All these too lie, whither a true form strays.
     Sweet when the lost arrive.
Foul sleet ices the twigs, the vision frays,
Festoons all signs; still as I come to name
My joy to you my joy springs up again the same, —
     The thaw alone delays, —
     Your letter came!

New Year's Eve

The grey girl who had not been singing stopped,
And a brave new no-sound blew through acrid air.
I set my drink down, hard. Somebody slapped
Somebody's second wife somewhere,
Wheeling away to long to be alone.
I see the dragon of years is almost done,
Its claws loosen, its eyes
Crust now with tears & lust and a scale of lies.

A whisky-listless and excessive saint
Was expounding his position, whom I hung
Boy-glad in glowing heaven: he grows faint:
Hearing what song the sirens sung,
Sidelong he web-slid and some rich prose spun.
The tissue golden of the gifts undone
Surpassed the gifts. Miss Weirs
Whispers to me her international fears.

Intelligentsia milling. In a semi-German
(Our loss of Latin fractured how far our fate, —
Disinterested once, linkage once like a sermon)
I struggle to articulate
Why it is our promise breaks in pieces early.
The Muses' visitants come soon, go surly
With liquor & mirrors away
In this land wealthy & casual as a holiday.

Whom the Bitch winks at. Most of us are linsey-
woolsey workmen, grandiose, and slack.
On m' analyse, the key to secrets. Kinsey
Shortly will tell us sharply back
Habits we stuttered. How revive to join
(Great evils grieve beneath: eye Caesar's coin)
And lure a while more home
The vivid wanderers, uneasy with our shame?

Priests of the infinite! ah, not for long.
The dove whispers, and diminishes
Up the blue leagues. And no doubt we heard wrong—
Wax of our lives collects & dulls; but was
What we heard hurried as we memorized,
Or brightened, or adjusted? Undisguised
We pray our tongues & fingers
Record the strange word that blows suddenly and
    lingers.

Imagine a patience in the works of love
Luck sometimes visits. Ages we have sighed,
And cleave more sternly to a music of
Even this sore word 'genocide'.
Each to his own! Clockless & thankless dream
And labour Makers, being what we seem.
Soon O enough we turn
Our tools in; brownshirt Time chiefly our works will
    burn.

I remember: white fine flour everywhere whirled
Ceaselessly, wheels rolled, a slow thunder boomed,
And there were snowy men in the mill-world
With sparkling eyes, light hair uncombed,
And one of them was humming an old song,
Sack upon sack grew portly, until strong
Arms moved them on, by pairs,
And then the bell clanged and they ran like hares.

Scotch in his oxter, my Retarded One
Blows in before the midnight; freezing slush
Stamps off, off. Worst of years! . . no matter, begone;
Your slash and spells (in the sudden hush)
We see now we had to suffer some day, so
I cross the dragon with a blessing, low,
While the black blood slows. Clock-wise,
We clasp upon the stroke, kissing with happy cries.

Of 1947

Narcissus Moving

Noise of the vans woke us before we would
At the second landing a fine mirror cracked
Scratches appeared on all the valued wood
And this was the Fairway's last official act

Unfit to form attachment he is flying
The weather favours jokers of this kind
News of the hairy cousins was supplying
Barkers with gossip not to speak his mind

Blond to the dawn comes down himself in green
Verging on joy   I see his knuckles white
With joy and yet he stood all night unseen
In reverie upstairs under the skylight

The neglected corners said what they were for
'Limpid the lapse & sweet relapse of water
Upon my trembling image, ah, no more'
He whispered and stole downstairs to the slaughter

With a bannister he laid a blue bone bare
A tongue tore hard but one boot in a groin
Sank like a drift   A double fist of hair
Like feathers members that will not rejoin

Flat slams below there but I blew my drag
Against my ash and strained, ash on the tile
Spoilt the good washroom, weary with a jag
I chinned the sill to watch a wicked mile

The walls of stone bury to some pavanne
The garden   A bloody rubbish a dancing shoe
'Two-Eyes could bear no more' like the dusty swan
Shut of its cage and doubtful what to do

A vile tune from the shattered radio
Incredibly arises & dies at once . .
A deeper silence, then we slowly know
Somewhere in the empty mansion one tap runs

'A Negress gnawed my lip up a terrible place
Why not? the rising sun will light me poor'
Only upon a young man's most blond face
Un silence de la mort de l'amour

The Dispossessed

'and something that . . that is theirs — no longer ours'
stammered to me the Italian page. A wood
seeded & towered suddenly. I understood. —

The Leading Man's especially, and the Juvenile Lead's,
and the Leading Lady's thigh that switches & warms,
and their grimaces, and their flying arms:

our arms, our story. Every seat was sold.
A crone met in a clearing sprouts a beard
and has a tirade. Not a word we heard.

Movement of stone within a woman's heart,
abrupt & dominant. They gesture how
fings really are. Rarely a child sings now.

My harpsichord weird as a koto drums
adagio for twilight, for the storm-worn dove
no more de-iced, and the spidery business of love.

The Juvenile Lead's the Leader's arm, one arm
running the whole bole, branches, roots, (O watch)
and the faceless fellow waving from her crotch,

Stalin-unanimous! who procured a vote
and care not use it, who have kept an eye
and care not use it, percussive vote, clear eye.

That which a captain and a weaponeer
one day and one more day did, we did, *ach*
we did not, *They* did . . cam slid, the great lock

lodged, and no soul of us all was near was near, —
an evil sky (where the umbrella bloomed)
twirled its mustaches, hissed, the ingenue fumed,

poor virgin, and no hero rides. The race
is done. Drifts through, between the cold black trunks,
the peachblow glory of the perishing sun

in empty houses where old things take place.

Venice, 182—

White & blue my breathing lady leans
across me in the first light, so we kiss.
The corners of her eyes are white. I miss.
renew. She means
to smother me thro' years of this.

Hell chill young widows in the heel of night —
perduring loves, melody's thrusting, press
flush with the soft skin, whence they sprung! back. Less
ecstasy might
save us for speech & politeness.

I hear her howl now, and I slam my eyes
against the glowing face. Foul morning-cheese
stands fair compared to love. On waspish knees
our pasts surprise
and plead us livid. Now she frees

a heavy lock was pulling . . I kiss it,
lifting my hopeless lids — and all trace
of passion's vanisht from her eyes & face,
the lip I bit
is bluer, a blackhead at the base

of her smooth nose looks sullenly at me,
we look at each other in entire despair,
her eyes are swimming by mine, and I swear
sobbing quickly
we are in love. The light hurts. 'There . .'

Scots Poem

Loversgrove lay
off to the lighthearted south,
chat-south, miles & more miles. Weel,
mot-tive flunks a man's mouth seems full of teeth.

Peered at her long
sidewise and would not or could
not say Love will be leaping
hopeless forever, hard on one who stood

near to her long
till she lookt poorly and died.
Braird in the breast evergreen,
grey the fieldgrass though, man's friend. I'm inside. —

— Trumpet shall sound,
angel & archangel cry
'Come forth, Isobel Mitchel,
and meet William Matheson in the sky.'

Sonnet 25

Sometimes the night echoes to prideless wailing
low, as I hunch home late & fever-tired
near you not, nearing the sharer I desired
toward whom till now I sailed back, but that sailing
yaws, from the cabin orders like a failing
dribble, the stores disordered & then fired
skid wild, the men are glaring, the mate has wired
'Hopeless'. Lockt in & humming, the Captain's nailing
a false log to the lurching table. Lies
& passion sing in the cabin on the voyage home,
the burgee should fly Jolly Roger. Wind
madness like the tackle of a crane — outcries
ascend — around to heave him from the foam
irresponsible, since all the stars rain blind.

Not To Live

It kissed us, soft, to cut our throats, this coast,
like a malice of the lazy King. I hunt,
& hunt! but find here what to kill? — nothing is blunt,
but phantoming uneases I find. Ghost
on ghost precedes of all most scared us, most
we fled. Howls fail upon this secret, far air: grunt,
shaming for food; you must. I love the King
& it was not I who strangled at the toast
but a flux of a free & dying adjutant:
God be with him. He & God be with us all,
for we are not to live. I cannot wring,
like laundry, blue my soul — indecisive thing . .
From undergrowth & over odd birds call
and who would starv'd so survive? God save the King.

They Have

A thing O say a sixteenth of an inch
long, with whiskers
& wings it doesn't use, & many legs,
has all this while been wandering in a tiny space
on the black wood table by my burning chair.
I see it has a feeler of some length
it puts out before it.
That must be how it was following the circuit
of the bottom of my wine-glass, vertical: Macon: I
    thought
it smelt & wanted some but couldn't get hold.
But here's another thing, on my paper, a fluff
of legs, and I blow: my brothers & sisters go away.
But here he's back, & got between the pad
& padback, where I save him and
shift him to my blue shirt, where he is.
The other little one's gone somewhere else.
They have things easy.

A Sympathy, A Welcome

Feel for your bad fall how could I fail,
poor Paul, who had it so good.
I can offer you only: this world like a knife.
Yet you'll get to know your mother
and humourless as you do look you will laugh
and all the others
will *not* be fierce to you, and loverhood
will swing your soul like a broken bell
deep in a forsaken wood, poor Paul,
whose wild bad father loves you well.

Note to Wang Wei

How could you be so happy, now some thousand years
dishevelled, puffs of dust?
It leaves me uneasy at last,
your poems teaze me to the verge of tears
and your fate. It makes me think.
It makes me long for mountains & blue waters.
Makes me wonder how much to allow.
(I'm reconfirming, God of bolts & bangs,
of fugues & bucks, whose rocket burns & sings.)
I wish we could meet for a drink
in a 'freedom from ten thousand matters'.
Be dust myself pretty soon; not now.